United States Congress

Amendment intended to be proposed by Mr. Stewart to the joint resolution

United States Congress

Amendment intended to be proposed by Mr. Stewart to the joint resolution

ISBN/EAN: 9783337150402

Printed in Europe, USA, Canada, Australia, Japan

Cover: Foto ©Suzi / pixelio.de

More available books at **www.hansebooks.com**

Thirty-Ninth Congress

First Session

Joint Committee on Reconstruction.

Journal.

Having compared the handwriting
in the Journal of Joint Com. on Reconstruction 39 cong, 1st & 2d sess. with the
handwriting of George A. Mark in the
records of the Library of Congress, I am
convinced that they are the same

T. J. Putnam

associate with said Mark for
years in Library of Congress.
(June 1910)

In the House of Representatives.

December 4, 1865.

On motion of _Mr. Stevens_:

Be it resolved, by the Senate and House of Representatives in Congress assembled: That a joint committee of fifteen members shall be appointed, nine of whom shall be members of the House, and six members of the Senate, who shall enquire into the condition of the States which formed the so-called Confederate States of America, and report whether they, or any of them, are entitled to be represented in either House of Congress, with leave to report at any time, by bill or otherwise; and until such report shall have been made, and finally acted on by Congress, no member shall be received into either House from any of the so-called Confederate States; and all papers relating to the representation of said States shall be referred to the said Committee without debate.

Attest

Edw'd. McPherson. Clerk.

December 12, 1865.

Amended in the Senate, on motion of _Mr. Anthony_, so as to read,

Resolved by the House of Representatives, (the Senate concurring) That a joint committee of fifteen members shall be appointed, nine of whom shall be members of the House, and six members of the Senate, who shall enquire into the condition of the States which formed the so-called Confederate States of America, and report whether they, or any of them, are entitled to be represented in either House of Congress, with leave to report at any time, by bill or otherwise.

111335

Attest.

J. W. Forney,
Secretary.

Dec. 13, 1865.

In the House of Representatives, on motion of <u>Mr. Stevens</u>, the amendments of the Senate were concurred in.

Attest,

Edw'd Mc Pherson.
Clerk.

Members on the part of the Senate.

- Mr. William P. Fessenden.   of   Maine.
  „   James W. Grimes,   „   Iowa.
  „   Ira Harris,   New York.
  „   Jacob M. Howard,   „   Ohio.
  „   Reverdy Johnson.   „   Maryland.
and   „   George H. Williams,   „   Oregon.

Members on the part of the House of Reps.

Mr. Thaddeus Stevens.   of   Penna.
  „   Elihu B. Washburne,   „   Illinois.
  „   Justin S. Morrill,   „   Vermont.
  „   Henry Grider.   „   Kentucky.
  „   John A. Bingham.   „   Ohio.
  „   Roscoe Conkling.   „   New York.
  „   George S. Boutwell,   „   Massachusetts.
  „   Henry T. Blow,   „   Missouri.
and   „   Andrew J. Rogers,   „   New Jersey.

Saturday, January 6th, 1866.

The Joint Committee on Reconstruction met (in the room of the Senate Committee on the Pacific Rail-road) pursuant to the call of Mr. Fessenden, its chairman.

Present – The Chairman, Messrs Grimes, Harris, Howard, Johnson and Williams, of the Senate, and

Messrs Stevens, Washburne, Morrill, Conkling, Boutwell and Blow, of the House.

On motion,

Ordered, That Mr. Wm. Blair Lord, (of New York City) be appointed clerk and stenographer of this Committee; and that the Chairman be instructed to obtain from the Senate the necessary authority for his employment.

On motion of Mr. Stevens;

Ordered that a sub-committee, to consist of three members, be appointed to wait on the President and request him to defer all further executive action in regard to reconstruction until this Committee shall have taken action on that subject.

On motion,

Ordered, That the Chairman, and Messrs Johnson and Washburne constitute said sub-committee.

Adjourned to ten A. M. on Tuesday next.

Tuesday, January 9. 1866.

The Committee met pursuant to adjournment: — all the members present.

The Chairman submitted the following resolution which was unanimously agreed to;

Resolved, That all the resolutions submitted to or adopted by this Committee, the views expressed in Committee by its different members, all votes taken and all other proceedings in Committee of whatever nature, be regarded by the members of the Committee and the clerk as of a strictly confidential character, until otherwise ordered.

The Chairman, from the sub-committee appointed, at the last meeting of the Committee, to wait on the President, reported orally,

That the Committee had waited on the President and expressed to him the views of the Committee as set forth in the resolution appointing the sub-committee; that the Committee desired to avoid all possible collision or misconstruction between the Executive and Congress in regard to the relative positions of Congress and the President, and that they thought it exceedingly desirable that, while this subject was under consideration by the joint Committee, no further action in regard to reconstruction should be taken by the President unless it should become imperatively necessary, and that they thought mutual respect would seem to require mutual forbearance on the part of the Executive and of Congress. To which the President replied substantially that while he considered it desirable that this matter of reconstruction should be advanced as rapidly as might be consistent with the public interest, still he desired to secure harmony of action between Congress and the Executive, and it was not his intention to do more than had been done, for the present.

Mr. Stevens submitted a joint resolution, upon which he asked immediate action by the Committee, proposing to submit for ratification to the several States the following amendment to the Constitution of the United States:

Representatives shall be apportioned among the several States, which may be included within this Union, according to the number of their respective legal voters; and for this purpose none shall be considered as legal voters who are not either natural born or naturalized citizens of the United States, of the age of twenty one years. Congress shall provide for ascertaining the number of said voters. A true census of the legal voters shall be taken at the same time with the regular census.

After discussion

Mr. Conkling moved to amend by inserting the word "male" between the word "naturalized" and the word "citizens".

The amendment was adopted.

Mr. Morrill moved to further amend by inserting after the words "of the age of twenty one years" the words "and who can read and write".

The amendment was not agreed to.

The further consideration of the subject was postponed till this evening.

The Chairman submitted the following:

Resolved that, in the opinion of this Committee, the insurgent States cannot, with safety to the rights of all the people of the United States, be allowed to participate in the Government until the basis of representation shall have been modified, and the rights of all persons amply secured, either by new provisions, or the necessary changes of existing provisions, in the Constitution of the United States, or otherwise

On motion of Mr. Stevens, the further consideration of the resolution was postponed

On motion of Mr. Stevens.

The Committee took a recess till 7½ o'clock this evening.

The Committee reassembled at 7½ o'clock P.M. — absent, Mr. Blow.

The consideration of the joint resolution submitted by Mr. Stevens was resumed.

Mr. Williams moved to further amend the same by striking out the words "and for this purpose none shall be considered as legal voters who are not either natural-born or naturalized male citizens of the United States, of the age of twenty one years."

After discussion,

Mr. Johnson moved to postpone the further consideration of the joint resolution until the next meeting of the Committee.

The motion was agreed to.

Mr. Stevens, and Mr. Howard, submitted propositions for the future consideration of the Committee.

Ordered, That the same be placed on file for future consideration.

On motion of Mr. Harris,

The Committee adjourned till Friday next at 10½ o'clock A.M.

Friday, January 12. 1866.

The Committee met pursuant to adjournment; absent Mr. Rogers.

The consideration of the joint resolution submitted by Mr. Stevens was resumed.

The pending question was upon the amendment proposed by Mr. Williams.

Mr. Williams withdrew his amendment.

5

Mr. Morrill moved the following as a substitute for the original proposition:

Representatives and direct taxes shall be apportioned among the several States, which may be included within this Union, according to their respective numbers of persons, deducting therefrom all of any race or color, whose members or any of them are denied any of the civil or political rights or privileges.

Mr. Williams gave notice that at the proper time he should move the following substitute;

Representatives and direct taxes shall be apportioned among the several States of the Union according to their respective numbers, including negroes, Indians, Chinese, and all persons, not white, who are not allowed the elective franchise by the Constitutions of the States in which they respectively reside.

Mr. Conkling gave a similar notice in regard to the following substitute;

Representatives and direct taxes shall be apportioned among the several States, which may be included within this Union, according to their respective numbers, counting the whole number of citizens of the United States; provided that whenever in any State civil or political rights or privileges shall be denied or abridged on account of race or color, all persons of such race or color shall be excluded from the basis of representation or taxation.

Mr. Boutwell gave a similar notice in regard to the following substitute:

Representatives and direct taxes shall be apportioned among the several States, which may be included within this Union, according to the respective number of citizens of the United States in each State; and no State shall make any distinction in the exercise of the elective franchise on account of race or color.

After discussion,

Mr. Bingham, in order to test the sense of the Committee, submitted the following resolution:

Resolved that, in the opinion of this Committee, the amendment to the Constitution of the United States submitted by Mr. Stevens, ought to be amended or modified.

Mr. Johnson moved as a substitute for the resolution of Mr. Bingham, the following:

Resolved, That, in the opinion of this Committee, the apportionment of representation in Congress, as now provided by the Constitution, ought to be changed.

Mr. Bingham accepted the substitute.

The question was then taken, by yeas and nays, on the resolution as modified, and it was decided in the affirmative. yeas 13, nay 1, not voting 1, as follows;

Yeas — The Chairman, Messrs Grimes, Harris, Howard, Johnson, Williams, Stevens, Washburne, Morrill, Bingham, Conkling, Boutwell and Blow: 13.

Nay — Mr. Grider. 1.

Not voting — Mr. Rogers. 1.

The resolution as modified was accordingly. adopted.

Mr. Johnson submitted the following resolution;

Resolved, That, in the opinion of this Committee, representatives should be apportioned among the several States according to their respective numbers of le-

Yeas — Messrs Grimes, Johnson, Stevens, Washburne, Bingham and Blow: 6.

Nays — The Chairman, Messrs Harris, Howard, Williams, Morrill, Grider, Conkling and Boutwell; 8

Absent and not voting, Mr. Rogers; 1.

So the resolution was not agreed to.

Mr. Morrill submitted the following:

Ordered, That a sub-committee, to consist of five members, including the Chairman of the Committee on the part of the Senate, and the Chairman of the Committee on the part of the House, (Messrs Fessenden and Stevens) be appointed, to which shall be referred the various propositions submitted by members of this Committee in relation to apportionment of representatives in Congress, with instructions to prepare and report to this Committee a proposition upon that subject.

The motion was agreed to.

Mr. Bingham submitted the following proposed amendment of the Constitution of the United States, and moved that the same be referred to the sub-committee just authorized:

The Congress shall have power to make all laws necessary and proper to secure to all persons in every state within this Union equal protection in their rights of life, liberty and property.

The motion was agreed to.

Mr. Stevens submitted the following proposed amendment of the Constitution, and moved that the same be referred to the sub-committee just author-

persons without regard to race or color.

The motion was agreed to.

On motion of Mr. Stevens,

Ordered, That the remaining members of the sub-committee, authorized at this meeting, be appointed by the Chairman of the Joint Committee.

The motion was agreed to.

The Chairman announced the following as members of the sub-committee

Messrs Fessenden and Stevens, (named in the order of the Joint Committee) and Messrs Howard, Conkling and Bingham.

On motion of Mr. Stevens;

Ordered, That the Chairman be instructed to introduce into the Senate a concurrent resolution authorizing the Joint Committee to send for persons and papers.

On motion of Mr. Bingham;

Ordered, That sub-committees, each composed of two members, be appointed to examine and report upon the present condition of the States composing the late so-called Confederate States of America, and not now represented in Congress; what has been their action in relation to any amendments of the Federal or State Constitutions; what may be the present legal position of the freedmen in the respective States; in what manner the so-called ordinances of secession have been treated; whether the validity of debts contracted for the support of the rebellion is acknowledged; and generally as to all evidence, documentary or otherwise, of the present loyalty or disloyalty upon the part of the people or governments of said states. That is to say, committees embracing

1st — Tennessee,

2 d – Virginia, North Carolina and South Carolina.

3 d – Georgia, Alabama, Mississippi and Arkansas.

and 4th – Louisiana, Florida and Texas.

On motion of Mr. Howard.

Ordered, That the sub-committees above authorized, be appointed by the Chairman of the Joint Committee.

On motion of Mr. Harris.

The Committee adjourned to 11 A.M. on Monday next.

———— ————

Monday, January 15. 1866.

The Committee met pursuant to adjournment; absent, Messrs Johnson and Blow.

On motion of Mr. Morrill;

Ordered, That the various sub-committees authorized on motion of Mr. Bingham, at the last meeting of the Committee, shall consist of three members each, instead of two members.

The Chairman announced the following as the members of the sub-committees ordered at the last meeting;

No. 1 – Messrs Grimes, Bingham and Crider.

" 2 – Howard, Conkling and Blow.

" 3 – Harris, Boutwell and Morrill.

" 4 – Williams, Washburne and Rogers.

Mr. Stevens submitted the following resolution of the House of Representatives.

Resolved, That all papers which may be offered relative to the representation of the late so-called Confederate States of America, or either of them, shall be referred to the Joint Committee of fifteen without debate; and no members shall be admitted from either of said so-called States until Congress shall believe such States, or either of them, entitled to representation."

Adjourned to meet on call of the Chairman.

Saturday, January 20. 1866.

The Committee met pursuant to call of its Chairman: — absent Mr. Johnson.

The Chairman laid before the Committee the following papers, which were ordered to be entered upon the Journal of the Committee;

In the Senate of the United States,
January 8, 1866.

On motion of Mr. Fessenden,

Ordered, That the Joint Committee to inquire into the condition of the States which formed the so-called Confederate States of America, be authorized to employ a stenographic clerk.

In the Senate of the United States,
January 12. 1866.

On motion of Mr. Fessenden,

Resolved by the Senate, the House of Representatives concurring, that the Joint Committee appointed to inquire into the condition of the States which formed the so-called Confederate States, be authorized to send for persons

Attest J. W. Forney,
Secretary.

In the House of Representatives,
January 16. 1866.

On motion of Mr. Stevens,

Resolved that the House concur in the foregoing resolution of the Senate.

Attest. Edw'd McPherson,
Clerk."

The Chairman, from the sub-committee on the basis of representation, reported that the sub-committee had directed him to report the following for the action of the joint Committee; the first two as alternative propositions, one of which, with the third proposition, to be recommended to Congress for adoption;

"Resolved, by the Senate and House of Representatives of the United States of America in Congress assembled, two-thirds of both Houses concurring, that the following Articles be proposed to the Legislatures of the several States, as amendments to the Constitution of the United States, which, when they, or either of them, shall be ratified by three-fourths of the said Legislatures, shall be valid as part of said Constitution; viz:

Article ___

Or the following:

Article—

Representatives and direct taxes shall be apportioned among the several States which may be included within this Union, according to their respective numbers, counting the whole number of citizens of the United States in each State; provided that, whenever the elective franchise shall be denied or abridged in any State on account of race, creed or color, all persons of such race, creed or color, shall be excluded from the basis of representation.

Article—

Congress shall have power to make all laws necessary and proper to secure to all citizens of the United States, in every State, the same political rights and privileges; and to all persons in every State equal protection in the enjoyment of life, liberty and property.

The Joint Committee proceeded to consider the report of the sub-committee.

Mr. Stevens moved that the last article be separated from whichever of the other two should be adopted by the Committee, and be considered by itself.

The question was taken by yeas and nays, and decided in the affirmative, yeas 10, nays 4, absent and not voting, 1, as follows:

Yeas — Messrs Grimes, Williams, Stevens, Washburne, Morrill, Bingham, Conk-

The question was taken by yeas and nays, and it was decided in the affirmative. yeas 11, nays 3. absent and not voting, 1—as follows;

Yeas— Messrs Grimes, Harris, Williams, Stevens, Washburne, Morrill, Bingham, Conkling, Boutwell, Blow and Rogers— 11.

Nays— The Chairman, Messrs Howard and Grider—3.

Absent and not voting— Mr. Johnson—1.

So the motion was agreed to.

Mr. Stevens moved to amend the proposed article by adding the following;

"And whenever the words "citizen of the United States", are used in the Constitution of the United States, they shall be construed to mean all persons born in the United States, or naturalized, excepting Indians."

Pending the consideration of which

Mr. Conkling moved to amend the proposed article by striking out the words "citizens of the United States in each State", and inserting in lieu thereof the words, "persons in each State, excluding Indians not taxed."

The question was taken by yeas and nays, and it was decided in the affirmative, yeas 11. nays 3, absent and not voting 1. as follows;

Yeas— Messrs Grimes, Harris, Howard, Williams, Washburne, Morrill, Grider, Conkling, Boutwell, Blow and Rogers— 11

Nays— The Chairman and Messrs Stevens and Bingham—3.

Absent and not voting— Mr. Johnson—1.

So the amendment was adopted.

The amendment was adopted.

Mr. Stevens withdrew his amendment.

The question was upon agreeing to the proposed article as amended, which was as follows;

"Representatives and direct taxes shall be apportioned among the several States which may be included within this Union, according to their respective numbers, counting the whole number of persons in each State, excluding Indians not taxed; provided that whenever the elective franchise shall be denied or abridged in any State on account of race or color, all persons of such race or color shall be excluded from the basis of representation."

The question was taken by yeas and nays, and it was decided in the affirmative, yeas 13, nay 1, absent and not voting 1— as follows;

Yeas — The Chairman, Messrs Grimes, Harris, Howard, Williams, Stevens, Washburne, Morrill, Grider, Bingham, Conkling, Boutwell and Blow — 13.

Nay — Mr. Rogers — 1.

Absent and not voting — Mr. Johnson — 1.

So the proposed article as amended was agreed to.

Pending the call of the yeas and nays

Messrs Howard and Grider each said, that although they voted in the affirmative, they desired to be understood as retaining their right to support, in their respective Houses, some proposition more in accordance with their views, should they deem it advisable to do so.

mittee (Mr. Stevens) be instructed to report as early as practicable to their respective Houses, the proposed amendment to the Constitution of the United States, this day agreed upon by the Joint Committee, and recommend its adoption by the same.

Mr. Rogers asked and obtained leave to submit to the House of Representatives a report setting forth the views of the minority of the Joint Committee upon the proposed amendment.

Adjourned to meet on call of the Chairman.

———— ————

Wednesday, January 24. 1866.

The Committee met pursuant to call of its Chairman: absent Messrs Harris and Johnson.

The Chairman laid before the Committee the following resolution of the Senate, which was ordered to be entered upon the Journal;

January 22, 1866.

Resolved, That until otherwise ordered, all papers presented to the Senate relating to the condition and title to representation of the so-called Confederate States, shall be referred to the Joint Committee upon that subject.

The Committee proceeded to the consideration of the following amendment to the Constitution proposed by the sub-committee on the basis of representation;

Congress shall have power to make all laws necessary and proper to secure to all citizens of the United States in each State the same political rights and privileges; and to all persons in every State equal protection in the enjoyment of life, liberty and property.

"political".

The question was taken by yeas and nays, and decided in the negative, yeas 2, nays 10, absent and not voting, 3, as follows;

Yeas — Messrs Howard and Rogers — 2.

Nays — The Chairman, Messrs Williams, Stevens, Washburne, Morrill, Grider, Bingham, Conkling, Boutwell and Blow — 10.

Absent and not voting — Messrs Grimes, Harris and Johnson.

So the amendment was not agreed to.

Mr. Boutwell moved to amend by striking out to and including the words "political rights and privileges", and inserting in lieu thereof the following;

"Congress shall have power to abolish any distinction in the exercise of the elective franchise in any State, which by law, regulation or usage may exist therein."

The amendment was not agreed to.

Mr. Blow moved to refer the proposed amendment to a select committee of three to be appointed by the chairman, with instructions to carefully review the same.

The question was taken by yeas and nays, and it was decided in the affirmative, yeas 7, nays 5, absent and not voting 3, as follows;

Yeas — The Chairman, Messrs Morrill, Grider, Conkling, Boutwell, Blow

Rogers.

On motion of <u>Mr. Stevens</u> it was

Ordered that the injunction of secrecy be removed so far as to allow any member of the Committee to announce in his place in Congress the substance and nature of the proposed amendment to the Constitution of the United States, under consideration by the Committee this morning.

Adjourned to meet on call of the Chairman.

—————— ——————

Saturday, January 27. 1866.

The Committee met pursuant to the call of its Chairman — absent Messrs Blow and Rogers.

<u>Mr. Bingham</u> from the sub-committee on the powers of Congress, reported back the proposed amendment of the Constitution ~~and~~ referred to them, in the following form;

"Congress shall have power to make all laws which shall be necessary and proper to secure all persons in every State full protection in the enjoyment of life, liberty and property; and to all citizens of the United States in any State the same immunities and also equal political rights and privileges."

The <u>Chairman</u> moved to strike out the word "also" in the last clause.

Mr. Johnson moved to strike out the last clause of the proposed amendment.

The question was taken by yeas and nays, and it was decided in the negative yeas 4, nays 6, absent and not voting 5, as follows;

Yeas — Messrs Harris. Johnson. Grider and Conkling — 4.

Nays — The Chairman, Messrs Williams, Stevens, Morrill. Bingham and Boutwell — 6.

Absent and not voting — Messrs Grimes, Howard. Washburne. Blow and Rogers — 5.

So the amendment was not agreed to.

Mr. Stevens moved that the Chairman be instructed to report the joint resolution as amended to the Senate, and recommend its adoption by Congress.

The question was taken by yeas and nays, and it was decided in the negative, yeas 5, nays 5, absent and not voting, 5, as follows;

Yeas — The Chairman, Messrs Williams, Stevens. Morrill and Bingham — 5.

Nays — Messrs Harris, Johnson. Grider, Conkling and Boutwell — 5.

Absent and not voting — Messrs Grimes, Howard. Washburne, Blow and Rogers — 5.

So the motion was not agreed to.

On motion of Mr. Stevens, the further consideration of the joint resolution was postponed until the next meeting of the Committee.

Adjourned to meet on call of the Chairman.

_____ _____

Washington, January 31. 1866.

The Committee met pursuant to the call of its Chairman — absent Mr. Washburne.

Mr. Stevens laid before the committee the joint resolution heretofore reported by the committee proposing an amendment to the Constitution of the United States in relation to the basis of representation, which, together with all propositions upon the same subject offered by members of the House were by order of the House again referred to this Committee without instructions.

The Committee proceeded to consider the joint resolution.

After discussion

Mr. Stevens moved to amend the same by striking out the words "and direct taxes."

The motion was agreed to, by yeas and nays as follows;

Yeas— The Chairman, Messrs Grimes, Harris, Howard, Johnson, Williams, Stevens, Morrill, Bingham, Conkling, Boutwell, and Blow.—12.

Nays— Messrs Grider and Rogers—2.

Absent and not voting— Mr. Washburne—1.

Mr. Johnson moved to amend the proviso so that it should read;

Provided that whenever the elective franchise shall be denied or abridged in any state, on account of race or color, in the election of the members of the most numerous branch of the State legislature, or in the election of the electors for President or Vice President of the United States, or members of Congress, all persons therein of such race or color shall be excluded from the basis of representation.

The motion was not agreed to.

Mr. Johnson submitted the following in order to obtain the sense of the Committee;

Resolved, That the proposed amendment to the Constitution of the United States, in relation to the basis of representation, should be so modified as to include among the grounds of disqualification therein referred to in relation to the elective franchise, one in

Ayes — The Chairman, Messrs Howard, Johnson, Williams, Grider and Blow — 6.

Nays — Messrs Grimes, Harris, Stevens, Morrill, Bingham, Conkling and Boutwell — 7.

Absent and not voting — Messrs Washburne and Rogers — 2.

So the motion was not agreed to.

Mr. Stevens moved that the joint resolution as modified be reported back to the House of Representatives, with a recommendation that the same do pass.

The question was taken by yeas and nays, and it was decided in the affirmative, yeas 10, nays 4, absent and not voting 1; as follows;

Yeas — Messrs Grimes, Harris, Howard, Williams, Stevens, Morrill, Bingham, Conkling, Boutwell and Blow — 10.

Nays — The Chairman, Messrs Johnson, Grider and Rogers — 4.

Absent and not voting — Mr. Washburne — 1.

The motion was accordingly agreed to.

Adjourned to meet on call of the Chairman.

——————— ———————

Saturday, February 3. 1866.

The Committee met pursuant to call of its Chairman — absent Messrs Johnson and Blow.

The Committee resumed the consideration of the proposed amendment of the Constitution of the United States, reported from the sub-committee on powers of Congress; the same having been amended, when last under consideration by the Committee (January 27, 1866) to read as follows;

'Congress shall have power to make laws which shall be necessary and proper to

and to citizens of the United States in every state the same immunities, and equal political rights and privileges.'

Mr. Bingham moved the following as a substitute, by way of amendment:

'The Congress shall have power to make all laws which shall be necessary and proper to secure to the citizens of each state all privileges and immunities of citizens in the several states; (Art. 4, Sec. 2) and to all persons in the several states equal protection in the rights of life, liberty and property, (5th Amendment.)'

After discussion,

The question was taken by yeas and nays, and it was determined in the affirmative, yeas 7, nays 6, absent and not voting 2, as follows;

Yeas — Messrs Howard, Williams, Washburne, Morrill, Bingham, Boutwell and Rogers — 7.

Nays — The Chairman, Messrs Grimes, Harris, Stevens, Grider, and Conkling — 6.

Absent and not voting — Messrs Johnson and Blow — 2.

So the amendment was agreed to.

The question was upon agreeing to the proposed amendment of the Constitution as amended.

The question was taken by yeas and nays, and it was determined in the affirmative, yeas 9, nays 4, absent and not voting 2, as follows;

Yeas — The Chairman, Messrs Grimes, Howard, Williams, Stevens, Washburne, Morrill, Bingham and Boutwell — 9.

Nays — Messrs Harris, Grider, Conkling, and Rogers — 4.

Absent and not voting — Messrs Johnson and Blow — 2.

So the proposition as amended was adopted.

The question was upon ordering the same to be reported to Congress for adoption.

On motion of Mr. Boutwell, the further consideration of the same was postponed for the present.

Mr. Howard submitted the following proposed amendment to the Constitution of the United States, for future consideration by the Committee;

"That the payment of every kind of indebtedness arising or growing out of the late rebellion, contracted or accruing in aid of it or in order to promote it, is forever prohibited to the United States and to each of the states; such indebtedness and all evidences thereof are hereby declared and in all courts and places shall be held and treated as in violation of this Constitution, and utterly void and of no effect".

Adjourned to meet on call of the Chairman.

Saturday, February 10. 1866.

The Committee met pursuant to the call of its Chairman — absent Mr. Washburne.

The Committee resumed the consideration of the joint resolution proposing an amendment to the Constitution of the United States, as amended on motion of Mr. Bingham at the last meeting.

Mr. Stevens moved that the same be reported to the two Houses of Congress.

The question was taken by yeas and nays, and it was decided in the affirmative, yeas 9. nays 5, absent and not voting 1, as follows;

Yeas — The Chairman. Messrs Grimes, Howard, Williams, Stevens, Morrill, Bingham, Boutwell and Blow — 9.

So the motion was agreed to.

Mr. Grider submitted the following resolution, the consideration of which was postponed till the next meeting of the Committee;

Resolved, That the sub-committee on the condition of Tennessee, as to loyalty, be requested to report to this Committee, with the proof taken touching that question, and that this Committee at its next meeting report to the House and Senate their conclusions and the evidence in the case.

Adjourned to meet on call of the Chairman.

———— ————

Thursday, February 15, 1866.

The Committee met pursuant to call of its Chairman — absent Mr. Johnson.

Mr. Bingham, from the sub-committee on Tennessee, submitted a report in writing with accompanying papers; also the following bill:

Whereas the people of Tennessee have presented a Constitution and asked admission into the Union, and which on due examination is found to be republican in its form of Government

Be it enacted by the Senate and House of Representatives of the United States of America in Congress assembled, that the State of Tennessee shall be one, and is hereby declared to be one of the United States of America, on an equal footing with the other states in all respects whatever.

Sec. 2 — And be it further enacted that until the Representatives in Congress shall be apportioned according to an actual enumeration of the inhabitants of the United States, the State of Tennessee shall be entitled to eight representatives in Con

After discussion, the further consideration of the same was postponed until the next meeting.

Adjourned to 11 A.M. on Saturday next.

———————— ————————

Washington, February 17. 1866.

The Committee met pursuant to adjournment — absent, Mr. Johnson.

The Committee resumed the consideration of the bill in relation to Tennessee, as set forth in the journal of the last meeting of the Committee.

Mr. Grimes moved to amend the preamble by inserting the word "Constitution" after the word "which".

The amendment was agreed to.

Mr. Stevens moved to amend the second section so that it would read as follows;

"Sec. 2 And be it further enacted that until the next congressional election the State of Tennessee shall be entitled to eight representatives."

The question was taken. by yeas and nays, and it was decided in the affirmative. yeas 9. nays 4. absent and not voting 2. as follows;

Ayes — The Chairman. Messrs Grimes, Howard, Stevens, Washburne, Morrill, Bingham, Conkling and Boutwell — 9.

Nays — Messrs Williams, Grider, Blow and Rogers — 4.

Absent and not voting — Messrs Harris and Johnson — 2.

So the amendment was agreed to.

Mr. Williams moved to strike out the second section as amended.

Resolved by the Senate and House of Representatives of the United States of America in Congress assembled; That the United States do hereby recognize the government of the State of Tennessee, inaugurated under a constitution adopted by a convention of the people of that State, on the 8th day of January, 1865, and ratified by a vote of the people at an election held on the 22d day of February, 1865, as the legitimate government of said state, under which said state is entitled to the guarantee and all other rights of a state government under the constitution of the United States.

Mr. Stevens, moved to amend the preamble of the bill reported from the sub-committee, by striking out the words "and asked admission into the Union."

Mr. Johnson here appeared in the committee room.

Mr. Bingham offered the following as a substitute for the bill of the sub-committee;

Whereas, The people of Tennessee did, on the 22d day of February, in the year of our Lord, 1865, adopt by a large popular vote an amended constitution of government, republican in form, and not inconsistent with the Constitution and laws of the United States, Therefore

Be it resolved, By the Senate and House of Representatives of the United States of America in Congress assembled, That the constitutional relations between Tennessee and the Government of the United States are hereby restored.

After discussion. Mr. Bingham submitted the following modification of his substitute;

United States.

And whereas the people of Tennessee are in a condition for restoration to the Union as a state, and have presented said constitutional government to Congress, and asked to be restored to their constitutional relations to the Government of the United States, Therefore,

Be it resolved by the Senate and House of Representatives of the United States of America, in Congress assembled, That the constitutional relations between Tennessee and the Government of the United States are hereby restored, and the said state of Tennessee, is declared to be a state in the Union on the same footing with the other states of the Union.

Mr. Harris withdrew his substitute.

The question was then taken, by yeas and nays, upon adopting the substitute of Mr. Bingham for the joint resolution reported from the sub-committee on Tennessee, as the basis of action for the joint committee, and it was decided in the affirmative, yeas 9, nays 4, absent or not voting 2, as follows;

Yeas—The Chairman, Messrs Grimes, Harris, Johnson, Williams, Washburne, Morrill, Bingham and Blow—9.

Nays—Messrs Howard, Stevens, Grider and Rogers—4.

Absent or not voting—Messrs Conkling and Boutwell—2.

So the substitute was adopted as the basis of action of the Committee.

Mr. Rogers moved the following;

Resolved, by the Senate and House of Representatives of the United States of America in Congress assembled, That the State of Tennessee is   of the states of and in this Union, with all the rights and privileges of the other states, and is entitled to her full representation in the Congress of the United States.

The same was rejected.

Mr. Williams moved that the whole subject of Tennessee be referred to a select committee of three members, to be appointed by the Chairman, and with instructions to report thereon to the joint committee at the next meeting

The question was taken, by yeas and nays, and it was decided in the affirmative, yeas 8, nays 7, as follows;

Yeas — The Chairman. Messrs Howard. Williams. Stevens, Washburne, Morrill, Conkling and Boutwell — 8.

Nays — Messrs Grimes, Harris, Johnson. Grider. Bingham. Blow and Rogers — 7.

So the motion was agreed to.

The Chairman appointed the following members as the select committee just ordered;

Messrs Williams. Conkling and Boutwell.

Adjourned till 10½ o'clock A. M. on Monday next.

——— ———

Monday, February 19. 1866.

The Committee met pursuant to adjournment; absent Mr. Johnson.

Mr. Conkling, from the select committee on Tennessee, appointed at the last meeting of the Committee, made a verbal report, and submitted the following as a substitute for the proposition of Mr. Bingham which was referred to the select committee;

Resolved by the Senate and House of Representatives of the United States of America in Congress assembled, that the functions and relations of Tennessee as a member of the Union are hereby declared to be established, and that Senators and

Representatives therefrom, their several elections, qualifications and returns being regular and sufficient, shall be entitled to admission.

And be it further resolved that the foregoing declaration is made upon the following fundamental conditions and guarantees;

First — The state of Tennessee shall never assume or pay any debt or obligation contracted or incurred in aid of the late rebellion, nor shall said state ever repudiate any debt or obligation contracted or incurred in aid of the Federal government against said rebellion; and said state shall be forever bound in like manner as the other states within this Union for the debt of the United States.

Second — The said state shall forever maintain in its constitution the provision therein contained disavowing the doctrine of secession.

Third — The said state shall, for not less than five years from the ratification of this resolution as hereinafter provided, exclude from the elective franchise, and from offices of honor, trust or profit, all those who adhered to and voluntarily gave aid or comfort to the late rebellion.

And be it further resolved, that the ratification of the foregoing conditions by a majority of the qualified electors of said state, in such manner as the legislature thereof may prescribe, shall be deemed an acceptance of this resolution; and upon a proclamation of such ratification by the President of the United States, the same shall become operative.

Mr. Bingham moved to strike out the third condition.

Mr. Boutwell moved to amend the second resolution by adding to it the

Pending the consideration of which,

The Chairman moved to amend the first condition of the second resolution by striking out all after the words "in aid of the late rebellion."

After discussion,

The Committee adjourned till 10½ A.M. to-morrow.

_____ _____

Tuesday, February 20. 1866.

The Committee met pursuant to adjournment — absent, Mr. Johnson.

The Committee resumed the consideration of the joint resolution in relation to Tennessee.

The pending question was upon the motion of the Chairman to amend the first condition of the second resolution, so that the same should read as follows:

"The State of Tennessee shall never assume or pay any debt or obligation contracted or incurred in aid of the late rebellion."

The question was taken by yeas and nays, and it was decided in the affirmative, yeas 8, nays 4, absent or not voting 3 as follows:

Yeas — The Chairman, Messrs Harris. Howard. Washburne. Morrill, Grider, Bingham and Rogers — 8.

Nays — Messrs Williams, Stevens, Conkling and Boutwell — 4.

Absent or not voting — Messrs Grimes, Johnson and Blow — 3.

So the amendment was agreed to.

The question then recurred upon the motion of Mr. Boutwell to still further amend the first resolution by adding the following condition:

"Fourth — Said state shall make no distinction in the exercise of the elective franchise on account of race or color.

The question was taken by yeas and nays, and it was decided in the negative, yeas 5, nays 6, absent or not voting 4, as follows:

Yeas — Messrs Howard, Stevens, Washburne, Morrill and Boutwell — 5.

Nays — Messrs Harris, Williams, Grider, Bingham, Conkling and Rogers — 6.

Absent or not voting — The Chairman, Messrs Grimes, Johnson and Blow — 4.

So the amendment was not agreed to.

Mr. Bingham moved the following as a substitute;

"Whereas, The people of Tennessee have presented a constitution to Congress, which constitution on due examination is found to be republican in its form of government, and the people are found to be in a condition to exercise the functions of a state, and can only exercise the same by the consent of the law-making power of the United States; Therefore

Be it enacted by the Senate and House of Representatives of the United States of America in Congress assembled, That the state of Tennessee is hereby declared to be one of the United States of America, on an equal footing with the other states in all respects whatever."

Pending the consideration of which,

Mr. Stevens said his opinions as to the expediency and propriety of this action on the part of the joint committee had been materially changed since yesterday. The first duty of the committee was to declare the power of Congress over this subject of reconstruction. He therefore moved to postpone all other business for the purpose of enabling him to offer the following concurrent resolution, which he should ask immediate ac-

Be it resolved by the House of Representatives, the Senate concurring, that in order to close agitation upon a question which seems likely to disturb the action of the government, as well as to quiet the uncertainty which is agitating the minds of the people of the eleven states which have been declared to be in insurrection, no senator or representative shall be admitted into either branch of Congress from any of said states until Congress shall have declared such state entitled to such representation.

After discussion, the question was taken by yeas and nays upon the motion to postpone, and it was decided in the affirmative, yeas 10, nays 4, absent 1, as follows;

Yeas — The Chairman, Messrs Grimes, Harris, Howard, Williams, Stevens, Washburne, Morrill, Conkling and Boutwell — 10.

Nays — Messrs Grider, Bingham, Blow and Rogers — 4.

Absent — Mr. Johnson — 1.

So the motion was agreed to.

Mr. Stevens submitted the foregoing concurrent resolution, and moved it be adopted and reported forthwith to the House of Representatives;

The question was taken by yeas and nays, and it was decided in the affirmative, yeas 12, nays 2, absent 1, as follows,

Yeas — The Chairman, Messrs Grimes, Harris, Howard, Williams, Stevens, Washburne, Morrill, Bingham, Conkling, Boutwell and Blow — 12.

Nays — Messrs Grider and Rogers — 2.

Absent — Mr. Johnson — 1.

So the resolution was adopted.

Saturday, March 3, 1866.

The Committee met pursuant to call of the Chairman, Absent Messrs Grimes, Howard and Blow.

The following resolution of the Senate was received and recorded:

February 20th 1866.

On motion by Mr. Wilson,

Resolved, That the Joint Committee on Reconstruction be directed to inquire into and report how far the states lately in rebellion, or any of them, have complied with the terms proposed by the President as conditions precedent to their resumption of practical relations with the United States; which terms and conditions were as follows; viz:

1st — That the several state constitutions should be amended by the insertion of a provision abolishing slavery.

2d — That the several state conventions should declare null and void the ordinances of secession and the laws and decrees of the Confederacy.

3d — That the several state legislatures should ratify the amendment to the Federal Constitution abolishing slavery.

4th — That the rebel debt, state and confederate, should be repudiated.

5th — That civil rights should be secured by laws applicable alike to whites and blacks.

The Committee resumed the consideration of the joint resolution concerning Tennessee.

Mr. Bingham modified the preamble of his substitute by inserting after the words 'the functions of a state', the words 'within this Union'; so that the same would read—'and the people are found to be in a condition to exercise the functions of a state within this Union', &c.

After discussion.

The question was taken upon the motion to substitute, and it was decided in the affirmative, yeas 7, nays 5, absent or not voting 3, as follows;

Yeas— Messrs Harris, Johnson, Stevens, Washburne, Grider, Bingham and Rogers—7.

Nays— The Chairman, Messrs Williams, Morrill, Conkling and Boutwell—5.

Absent or not voting— Messrs Grimes, Howard and Blow—3.

So the motion to substitute was agreed to.

Mr. Johnson moved to amend the substitute by striking out of the preamble the last clause as follows;

"And can only exercise the same by the consent of the law-making power of the United States."

After discussion.

The question was taken by yeas and nays, and it was decided in the negative, yeas 4, nays 7, absent or not voting 4, as follows;

Yeas— Messrs Harris, Johnson, Grider, and Rogers—4.

Nays— The Chairman, Messrs Williams, Stevens, Washburne, Morrill, Bingham and Boutwell—7.

Absent or not voting— Messrs Grimes, Howard, Conkling and Blow—4.

So the motion to strike out was not agreed to.

Mr. Blow entered the Committee-room about this time.

The Chairman stated that he had just received a note from Mr. Grimes, stating that he was absent on account of indisposition, and requesting the Chairman to cast his vote for him on all questions before the Committee.

The question was upon adopting the preamble and bill substituted for the joint resolution of the select committee, on motion of Mr. Bingham.

During the discussion thereon,

The Chairman read a preamble and resolution in relation to Tennessee, which he had drawn up, but stated that he would not offer it for the action of the Committee.

Mr. Bingham said he would, with the consent of the Committee, modify his preamble, in accordance with what the Chairman had read, and also change the form of the bill so as to make it a joint resolution.

Leave was granted and the preamble and bill of Mr. Bingham was modified as follows;

"Whereas the people of Tennessee have made known to the Congress of the United States their desire that the constitutional relations heretofore existing between them and the United States may be fully established, and did, on the 22d day of February, 1865, by a large popular vote, adopt and ratify a constitution of government, republican in form, and not inconsistent with the Constitution and laws of the United States, and a state government has been organized under the provisions thereof, which said provisions and the laws passed in pursuance thereof proclaim and denote loyalty to the Union;

the consent of the law-making power of the United States; Therefore be it

Resolved, by the Senate and House of Representatives of the United States of America in Congress assembled, That the State of Tennessee is hereby declared to be one of the United States of America, on an equal footing with the other states in all respects whatever."

The question was upon adopting the preamble and joint resolution as modified.

Mr. Harris and Mr. Conkling called for a division of the question.

The question was first taken, by yeas and nays, upon agreeing to the joint resolution, and it was decided in the affirmative, yeas 8, nays 4, absent or not voting 3, as follows;

Yeas— Messrs Harris, Johnson, Williams, Stevens, Grider, Bingham, Blow and Rogers—8.

Nays— The Chairman, Messrs Washburne, Morrill, and Boutwell—4.

Absent, or not voting— Messrs Grimes, Howard and Conkling—3.

So the joint resolution was agreed to.

The question was then taken, by yeas and nays, upon agreeing to the preamble, and it was decided in the affirmative, yeas 7, nays 5, absent, or not voting 3, as follows;

The Chairman asked to have the votes of Mr. Grimes recorded, in accordance with his request in a note to the chairman.

Mr. Rogers objected, and the votes were recorded and the results announced as above.

Mr. Bingham moved that the preamble and joint resolution, together with the memorial, accompanying papers and testimony relating to Tennessee, be reported to the House of Representatives.

Mr. Conkling moved to amend the motion of Mr. Bingham by adding that all the testimony taken by sub-committees in relation to the states which have been declared to be in insurrection, which may be ready for publication, be also reported to Congress and its printing recommended.

After discussion

The question was taken upon the amendment of Mr. Conkling, and upon a division there were ayes 4, noes 6.

So the amendment was not agreed to.

The motion of Mr. Bingham was then agreed to.

Mr. Conkling and Mr. Rogers severally asked and obtained leave to submit

Nays— Messrs Johnson. Grider and Rogers— 3.

Absent or not voting— Messrs Grimes. Howard and Morrill— 3.

So the motion was agreed to.

Adjourned to meet on call of the Chairman.

———— ————

Washington. March 5, 1866.

The Committee met pursuant to the call of its Chairman — absent Messrs Howard and Blow.

Mr. Bingham moved to reconsider the vote by which the Committee agreed to the joint resolution in relation to Tennessee, and directed the same to be reported to the House of Representatives.

The motion to reconsider was agreed to.

Mr. Bingham moved to amend the joint resolution by striking out at the close the words "in all respects whatever", and adding to the resolution the following;

"upon the express condition that the people of Tennessee will maintain and enforce in good faith their existing constitution and laws excluding those who have been engaged in rebellion against the United States from the exercise of the elective franchise for the respective periods of time therein provided for, & shall also exclude for like periods of time the same persons from eligibility to office."

Mr. Stevens moved to amend the amendment by addition as follows;

"which conditions shall be ratified by the legislature of Tennessee, or the people thereof as the legislature may direct before this act shall take effect".

The question was taken by yeas and nays, upon the amendment to the amendment, and it was decided in the affirmative, yeas 8, nays 5, absent or not voting 2.

Yeas — The Chairman. Messrs Grimes, Williams, Stevens, Washburne, Morrill, Conkling and Boutwell — 8.

Nays — Messrs Harris, Johnson, Grider, Bingham and Rogers — 5.

Absent or not voting — Messrs Howard and Blow — 2.

So the amendment to the amendment was agreed to.

The question was then taken, by yeas and nays, upon the amendment as amended, and it was decided in the affirmative, yeas 10, nays 3, absent or not voting 2, as follows;

Yeas — The Chairman, Messrs Grimes, Harris, Williams, Stevens, Washburne, Morrill, Bingham, Conkling and Boutwell — 10.

Nays — Messrs Johnson, Grider and Rogers — 3.

Absent and not voting — Messrs Howard and Blow — 2.

So the amendment as amended was agreed to.

Mr Conkling moved to further amend the joint resolution by inserting before the part adopted on motion of Mr. Stevens the following;

"and the state of Tennessee shall never assume or pay any debt or obligation contracted or incurred in aid of the late rebellion; nor shall said state ever in any manner claim from the United States or make any allowance or compensation for slaves emancipated or liberated in any way whatever."

The question was taken, by yeas and nays, and it was decided in the affirm

39

So the amendment was agreed to.

Mr. Stevens moved to further amend the preamble and joint resolution by transferring the enacting clause from just before the joint resolution to the beginning of the preamble;

The question was taken, by yeas and nays, and it was decided in the affirmative, yeas 10, nays 3, absent 2, as follows;

Yeas — Chairman, Messrs Grimes, Harris, Williams, Stevens, Washburne, Morrill, Bingham, Conkling and Boutwell — 10.

Nays — Messrs Johnson, Grider and Rogers — 3.

Absent or not voting — Messrs Howard and Blow — 2.

So the motion of Mr. Stevens was agreed to.

Mr. Harris moved to strike out the following words;

"and can only exercise the same by the consent of the law making power of the United States".

The question was taken, by yeas and nays, and it was decided in the negative, yeas 5, nays 8, absent and not voting 2, as follows;

Yeas — The Chairman, Messrs Harris, Johnson, Grider and Rogers — 5.

Nays — Messrs Grimes, Williams, Stevens, Washburne, Morrill, Bingham, Conkling, and Boutwell — 8.

Absent and not voting — Messrs Howard and Blow — 2.

The question was then taken, by yeas and nays, upon agreeing to the joint resolution as amended, and directing the same to be reported to the House of Representatives, and it was decided in the affirmative, yeas 8, nays 5, absent and not

ham and Conkling 8.

Nays — Messrs Johnson. Washburne, Grider, Boutwell and Rogers — 5.

Absent or not voting — Messrs Howard and Blow — 2.

So the joint resolution was adopted and ordered to be reported to the House of Representatives.

Adjourned to meet on call of the Chairman.

———— ————

Washington. April 16, 1866.

The Committee met pursuant to the call of the Chairman — Absent Messrs Fessenden Harris, Grider, Conkling. Boutwell and Blow.

Mr. Morrill stated that he called on Mr. Fessenden yesterday, and found him confined to his bed by illness, and under the care of a physician.

Mr. Stevens (Chairman of the House portion of the Committee) took the chair and called the Committee to order.

The object of the meeting was stated to be to hear Mr. Stewart, Senator from the State of Nevada, explain the purpose and effect of the joint resolution introduced by him in the Senate of the United States, on the 12th instant, being entitled "Joint Resolution (S.R. 62) proposing an amendment to the Constitution of the United States; also setting forth certain conditions upon which the states, the people of which have been lately in insurrection against the United States, shall be restored to their representation in Congress."

Mr. Stewart proceeded to address the Committee at length in support and advocacy of his resolution.

After he had concluded,

On motion of Mr. Grimes,

The Committee adjourned to 11 A. M. on Saturday next.

——— ———

Washington, April 21. 1866.

The Committee met pursuant to adjournment — absent. The Chairman, and Messrs Harris and Conkling.

Mr. Stevens moved that Mr. Johnson take the chair in absence of the Chairman.

The motion was agreed to.

Mr. Grimes stated that Mr. Fessenden was recovering, and would probably be out next week.

On motion of Mr. Stevens it was

Resolved, That in the opinion of this Committee it is expedient that the taking of testimony by the several sub-committees be concluded next week.

Mr. Stevens said he had a plan of reconstruction, one not of his own framing, but which he should support, and which he submitted to the Committee for consideration.

It was read as follows;

✓ A joint resolution proposing an amendment to the Constitution, and to provide for the restoration to the States lately in insurrection of their full political rights.

Whereas it is expedient that the States lately in insurrection should, at the earliest day consistent with the future peace and safety of the Union be restor-

States of America in Congress assembled, (two-thirds of both Houses concurring) that the following Article be proposed to the Legislatures of the several states as an amendment to the Constitution of the United States, which, when ratified by three-fourths of said Legislatures, shall be valid as part of the Constitution, namely:

Article —

Section 1 — No discrimination shall be made by any state, nor by the United States, as to the civil rights of persons because of race, color, or previous condition of servitude.

Sec. 2 — From and after the fourth day of July, in the year one thousand eight hundred and seventy six, no discrimination shall be made by any state nor by the United States as to the enjoyment by classes of persons of the right of suffrage, because of race, color, or previous condition of servitude.

Sec. 3 — Until the fourth day of July, one thousand eight hundred and seventy six, no class of persons, as to the right of any of whom to suffrage discrimination shall be made by any state, because of race, color, or previous condition of servitude, shall be included in the basis of representation:

Sec. 4 — Debts incurred in aid of insurrection or of war against the Union, and claims of compensation for loss of involuntary service or labor, shall not be paid by any state nor by the United States.

Sec. 5 — Congress shall have power to enforce, by appropriate legislation, the provisions of this article.

in conformity with the first section thereof, the Senators and Representatives from such state, if found duly elected and qualified, shall, after having taken the usual oath of office, be admitted as such;

Provided, that no person who, having been an officer in the army or navy of the United States, or having been a member of the Thirty Sixth Congress, or of the Cabinet in the year one thousand eight hundred and sixty, took part in the late insurrection, shall be eligible to either branch of the national legislature until after the fourth day of July, one thousand eight hundred and seventy six.

Mr. Stevens said he had submitted the proposed amendment to the Constitution with the proposed legislation by Congress, to the Committee for action together; but it would be necessary to submit the two propositions separately to Congress for its action.

The Committee then proceeded to consider the same.

The question was upon agreeing to the proposed first section of the amendment.

Mr. Bingham moved to amend the same by adding the following;

"nor shall any state deny to any person within its jurisdiction the equal protection of the laws, nor take private property for public use without just compensation."

After discussion thereon

The question was taken, and it was decided in the negative, yeas 5, nays 7, absent 3, as follows;

Boutwell — 7.

Absent — Messrs Fessenden, Harris and Conkling — 3.

So the amendment was not agreed to.

The question was taken upon adopting the first section, and it was decided in the affirmative, yeas 10, nays 2, absent 3 as follows;

Yeas — Messrs Grimes, Howard, Johnson, Williams, Stevens, Washburne, Morrill, Bingham, Boutwell and Blow — 10.

Nays — Messrs Grider and Rogers — 2.

Absent — Messrs Fessenden, Harris and Conkling — 3.

The first section was accordingly adopted.

The question was upon adopting the second section.

After discussion thereon

The question was taken, and it was decided in the affirmative, yeas 8, nays 4, absent 3, as follows;

Yeas — Messrs Grimes, Harris, Williams, Stevens, Washburne, Morrill, Bingham and Blow — 8.

Nays — Messrs Johnson, Grider, Boutwell and, Rogers — 4.

Absent — Messrs Fessenden, Harris and Conkling — 3.

So the second section was adopted.

The question was then taken upon adopting the third section, and it was decided in the affirmative, yeas 9, nays 3, absent 3, as follows;

Yeas — Messrs Grimes, Howard, Williams, Stevens, Washburne, Morrill, Bing=

So the third section was adopted.

The question was upon adopting the fourth section.

Mr. Rogers moved to amend by striking out the words, "by any state nor", so that the clause would read — "shall not be paid by the United States".

The question was taken, and it was decided in the negative, yeas 3, nays 9, absent 3 as follows:

Yeas — Messrs Johnson, Grider and Rogers — 3.

Nays — Messrs Grimes, Howard, Williams, Stevens, Washburne, Morrill, Bingham, Boutwell and Blow — 9.

Absent — Messrs Fessenden, Harris and Conkling — 3.

So the amendment was not agreed to.

Mr. Stevens moved to amend the section by inserting after the word "debts" the words "or obligations already incurred, or which may hereafter be"; so that it would read — "Debts or obligations already incurred, or which may hereafter be incurred in aid of insurrection", &c.

The amendment was agreed to.

The question was taken upon the section as amended, and it was decided in the affirmative, yeas 10, nays 2, absent 3, as follows:

Yeas — Messrs Grimes, Howard, Johnson, Williams, Stevens, Washburne, Morrill, Bingham, Boutwell and Blow — 10.

Nays — Messrs Grider and Rogers — 2.

Absent — Messrs Fessenden, Harris and Conkling — 3.

So the fourth section as amended was adopted.

Mr. Bingham moved to insert as section five the following:

"Sec. 5 No state shall make or enforce any law which shall abridge the privileges or immunities of citizens of the United States; nor shall any state deprive any person of life, liberty or property without due process of law, nor deny to any person within its jurisdiction the equal protection of the laws."

After discussion thereon

The question was taken, and it was decided in the affirmative, yeas 10, nays 2, absent 3, as follows;

Yeas — Messrs Grimes, Howard, Johnson, Williams, Stevens, Washburne, Morrill, Bingham, Boutwell and Blow — 10.

Nays — Messrs Grider and Rogers — 2.

Absent — Messrs Fessenden, Harris and Conkling — 3.

So the section proposed by Mr. Bingham was adopted.

The sixth section was read, giving Congress power to enforce the provisions of the article.

The question was taken upon adopting the section, and it was decided in the affirmative, yeas 10, nays 2, absent 3, as follows;

Yeas — Messrs Grimes, Howard, Johnson, Williams, Stevens, Washburne, Morrill, Bingham, Boutwell and Blow — 10.

Nays — Messrs Grider and Rogers — 2.

Absent — Messrs Fessenden, Harris and Conkling — 3.

So the sixth section was adopted.

The Committee proceeded to consider the accompanying joint resolution.

Mr. Morrill submitted the following additional resolution;

"And be it further resolved, That when any state lately in insurrection shall have adopted Article ____ of amendment to the Constitution as proposed ____ ,

due and unpaid in such state, may be assumed and paid by such state; and the payment thereof, upon proper assurances from such state to be given to the Secretary of the Treasury of the United States, may be postponed for a period not exceeding ten years."

Pending which

Mr. Bingham moved to amend the resolution submitted by Mr. Stevens by striking out after the enacting clause the following words;

"That whenever the above recited amendment shall have become part of the Constitution, and any state lately in insurrection shall have ratified the same, and shall have modified its constitution and laws in conformity with the first section thereof" —

And inserting in lieu thereof the following:

"That whenever, after the first day of February, 1867, any state lately in insurrection shall have adopted this article of amendment, and shall have conformed its constitution thereto and to the constitution and laws of the United States, such state shall be entitled to representation in the Congress of the United States, and"

Mr. Conkling at this period of the session entered the committee room, and stated that he had been unable to come earlier.

After some discussion upon the amendment proposed by Mr. Bingham

On motion of Mr. Grimes it was

Ordered that when the Committee adjourn to-day it be to meet at 10 A. M. on Monday next.

The Committee adjourned.

———————   ———————

Washington April 23, 1866.

The Committee met pursuant to adjournment, (Mr. Johnson in the chair) Absent Messrs Fessenden, Harris and Grider.

The Committee resumed the consideration of the joint resolution pending at the adjournment on Saturday.

Mr. Stevens said he desired to withdraw the joint resolution submitted by him on Saturday, so far as the same related to the admission of the states lately in insurrection, for the purpose of submitting a bill in its place — leaving the proposed amendment to the Constitution to stand by itself, as it had been adopted by the Committee.

Mr. Howard moved that Mr. Stevens have the leave asked.

The motion was agreed to, and the joint resolution was accordingly withdrawn.

Mr. Stevens submitted the following bill for the consideration of the Committee.

A Bill to provide for the restoration to the states lately in insurrection of their full political rights.

Whereas it is expedient that the states lately in insurrection should, at the earliest day consistently with the future peace and safety of the Union, be restor-

"Article —

Section 1 — No discrimination shall be made by any state nor by the United States as to the civil rights of persons because of race, color or previous condition of servitude.

Sec. 2 — From and after the fourth day of July in the year 1876 no discrimination shall be made by any state nor by the United States, as to the enjoyment, by classes of persons, of the right of suffrage, because of race, color, or previous condition of servitude.

"Sec. 3 — Until the fourth day of July, 1876, no class of persons, as to the right of any of whom to suffrage discrimination shall be made by any state, because of race, color or previous condition of servitude, shall be included in the basis of representation.

"Sec. 4 — Debts or obligations already incurred or which may hereafter be incurred in aid of insurrection or of war against the Union, and claims for compensation for loss of involuntary service or labor, shall not be paid by any state nor by the United States.

"Sec. 5 — No state shall make or enforce any law which shall abridge the privileges or immunities of citizens of the United States; nor shall any state deprive any person of life, liberty or property without due process of law; nor deny to any person within its jurisdiction the equal protection of the laws.

"Sec. 6 — The Congress shall have power to enforce by appropriate legislation the provisions of this article."

Now, Therefore,

of the United States of America in Congress assembled: That whenever the above recited amendment shall have become part of the Constitution, and any state lately in insurrection shall have ratified the same, and shall have modified its constitution and laws in conformity with the first section thereof, the Senators and Representatives from such state, if found duly elected and qualified, shall after having taken the usual oath of office, be admitted into Congress as such; Provided, That until after the fourth day of July, 1876, no person shall be eligible to either branch of the National Legislature who is included in any of the following classes; namely;

First—Persons who having been officers of the army or navy of the United States, or having been members of the 36th Congress, or having held in the year 1860 seats in the Cabinet, or judicial offices under the United States, did afterwards take part in the late insurrection.

Second—Persons who have been civil or diplomatic officers of the so-called confederate government, or officers of the army or navy of said government above the rank of colonel in the army and of lieutenant in the navy.

Third—Persons in regard to whom it shall appear that they have treated officers or soldiers or sailors of the army or navy of the United States, of whatever race, or color, captured during the late civil war otherwise than lawfully as prisonto, said state shall be entitled to representation in Congress; and upon the ratification in good faith by the other states lately in insurrection of the foregoing article of amendment said states shall after the first day of February, 1867, be entitled to representation in Congress, subject to the following condition, that said states so ratifying said amendment shall conform their constitutions and laws thereto; Provided, however."

The question was taken upon the amendment, and it was decided in the negative, yeas 4, nays 8, absent 3, as follows;

Yeas — Messrs Johnson, Bingham, Blow and Rogers — 4.

Nays — Messrs Grimes, Howard, Williams, Stevens, Washburne, Morrill, Conkling and Boutwell — 8.

Absent — Messrs Fessenden, Harris and Grider — 3.

So the amendment was rejected.

Mr Stevens moved to amend the second clause of exceptions by striking out the words "civil or."

The amendment was agreed to.

Mr. Stevens moved to further amend the same clause by striking out the word "lieutenant" and inserting the word "master".

The amendment was agreed to.

Mr. Williams moved to strike out the fourth clause as follows;

"Fourth — Persons in regard to whom it shall appear that they are disloyal."

Yeas— Messrs Grimes, Howard, Johnson, Williams, Stevens, Washburne, Morrill, Bingham, Conkling, Boutwell, Blow, and Rogers— 12.

Nays— 0.

Absent— Messrs Fessenden, Harris and Grider—3.

So the motion to strike out was agreed to.

Mr. Boutwell moved to strike out all after the words "in any of the following classes, namely," and to insert in lieu thereof the following;

First— The President and Vice President of the Confederate States of America so-called, the heads of departments and the members of both houses of the Congress thereof.

Second— Those who in other countries have acted as agents of the Confederate States of America so called.

Third— Heads of departments in the government of the United States, Judges of the Courts of the United States, officers of the army and navy of the United States, and members of either house of the Congress of the United States, who aided the late rebellion.

Fourth— Those who acted as officers of the Confederate States of America so-called, above the grade of colonel in the army or master in the navy, and any one who as governor of either of said so-called Confederate States gave aid or comfort to the rebellion.

Fifth— Those who have treated officers or soldiers or sailors of the army or navy of the United States, captured during the late war, otherwise than lawfully as prisoners of war."

After discussion,

The question was taken, and it was decided in the affirmative, yeas 8, nays 4, absent

3, as follows:

Yeas — Messrs Grimes, Howard, Williams, Stevens, Washburne, Morrill, Conkling and Boutwell — 8.

Nays — Messrs Johnson, Bingham, Blow and Rogers — 4.

Absent — Messrs Fessenden, Harris and Grider — 3.

So the amendment was agreed to.

<u>Mr. Boutwell</u> moved to further amend by striking out after the words "Provided, That", the words — "until after the fourth day of July, 1876."

After discussion,

The question was taken, and it was decided in the affirmative, yeas 7. nays 5, absent 3, as follows:

Yeas — Messrs Grimes, Howard, Stevens, Washburne, Conkling, Boutwell and Rogers — 7.

Nays — Messrs Johnson, Williams, Morrill, Bingham and Blow — 5.

Absent — Messrs Fessenden, Harris and Grider — 3.

So the amendment was agreed to.

<u>Mr. Morrill</u> moved the following as an additional section:

"Sec. 2 — And be it further enacted, That when any state lately in insurrection shall have ratified the foregoing proposed amendment to the Constitution, any part of the direct tax under the act of August 5, 1861, which may remain due and unpaid in such state, may be assumed and paid by such state; and the payment thereof, upon proper assurances from such state, to be given to the Secretary of the Treasury of the United States, may be postponed for a period not exceeding ten years from and after the passage of this act."

After discussion,

The question was taken, and it was decided in the affirmative, yeas 11, nays 1. absent 3, as follows;

Yeas — Messrs Grimes, Howard, Johnson. Williams, Stevens, Washburne, Morrill, Bingham, Conkling, Boutwell and Blow — 11.

Nay — Mr. Rogers — 1.

Absent — Messrs Fessenden. Harris and Grider — 3.

So the additional section was adopted.

Mr. Washburne moved that the chairmen of the Senate and House portions of the joint committee (Messrs Fessenden and Stevens) be instructed to report the joint resolution and bill agreed upon by the Committee to their respective houses; and that they ask permission to submit reports upon the same at some future time.

Mr. Grimes moved to amend the motion of Mr. Washburne, by striking out the last clause and inserting in lieu thereof the following;

"And that they be instructed to prepare reports to accompany the same."

Mr. Rogers asked leave for the minority of the Committee to prepare and submit their views in the shape of reports.

Pending which,

Mr. Conkling moved that when the Committee adjourn to-day, it be to meet on Wednesday next at 10½ o'clock A. M.

The question was taken, and it was decided in the affirmative, yeas 8, nays 4. absent 3. as follows;

Yeas — Messrs Grimes, Howard, Johnson, Williams, Morrill, Conkling, Boutwell and Blow — 8.

So the motion was agreed to.

Mr Conkling moved that the Committee now adjourn.

The question was taken, and it was decided in the affirmative, yeas 8, nays 4. absent 3, as follows;

Yeas—Messrs Grimes, Howard, Johnson, Williams, Morrill, Conkling, Boutwell and Blow—8.

Nays—Messrs Stevens, Washburne, Bingham and Rogers—4.

Absent—Messrs Fessenden, Harris and Grider—3.

So the motion was agreed to, and the Committee accordingly adjourned.

——— ———

Washington, April 25, 1866.

The Committee met pursuant to adjournment (Mr. Johnson in the chair) Absent—Messrs Fessenden and Washburne.

The question pending at the adjournment of the last meeting was the motion of Mr. Washburne instructing the chairmen of the Senate and House portions of the joint committee to report to their respective houses the joint resolution and bill agreed upon by the Committee at its last meeting, and to ask leave to submit written reports at some future time to accompany the same.

To this motion Mr. Grimes had moved an amendment; viz: to strike out the last clause and to insert an instruction to prepare reports to accompany

Mr. Conkling moved to amend the bill by striking out the word "usual" before the words "oath of office", and inserting in lieu thereof the word "required".

The amendment was agreed to.

Mr. Bingham moved further to amend the bill by striking out the word "oath" and inserting the word "oaths."

The amendment was agreed to.

Mr. Williams moved to amend the joint resolution by striking out the fifth section of the proposed amendment to the Constitution, as follows:

"Section 5 — No state shall make or enforce any law which shall abridge the privileges or immunities of citizens of the United States; nor shall any state deprive any person of life, liberty, or property without due process of law; nor deny to any person within its jurisdiction the equal protection of the laws."

After discussion

The question was taken, and it was decided in the affirmative, yeas 7 nays 5, absent or not voting 3, as follows:

Yeas — Messrs Harris, Howard, Johnson, Williams, Grider, Conkling and Boutwell — 7.

Nays — Messrs Stevens, Morrill, Bingham, Rogers and Blow — 5.

Absent, or not voting — Messrs Fessenden, Grimes and Washburne — 3.

So the amendment was agreed to.

The question recurred upon the motion of Mr. Washburne to report the joint resolution and bill agreed upon to the two houses, &c.

After discussion,

Yeas— Messrs Grimes, Harris, Howard, Williams, Stevens, Morrill, and Bingham—7.

Nays— Messrs Johnson, Grider, Conkling, Boutwell, Blow and Rogers—6.

Absent— Messrs Fessenden and Washburne—2.

So the motion was agreed to.

Mr. Bingham submitted for adoption by the Committee as a separate article of amendment to the Constitution, the section which had been stricken out of the one adopted by the Committee.

After discussion,

The question was taken, and it was decided in the negative, yeas 4, nays 8, absent or not voting 3, as follows;

Yeas— Messrs Johnson, Bingham, Grider and Rogers—4.

Nays— Messrs Grimes, Howard, Williams, Stevens, Morrill, Conkling, Boutwell and Blow—8.

Absent, or not voting— Messrs Fessenden, Harris and Washburne—3.

So the proposition of Mr. Bingham was not agreed to.

Mr. Grider gave notice that at the proper time he should submit for the consideration and action of the Committee the following resolution;

Resolved, That, in the opinion of this Committee, the people of Tennessee having elected according to law loyal men as Senators and Representatives, they should be admitted to seats in the present Congress, upon taking the usual oath of office.

Mr. Williams moved to reconsider the vote by which the Committee directed the joint resolution and bill adopted by the Committee to be reported to the two houses of Congress.

The question was taken, and it was decided in the affirmative, yeas 10, nays 2, absent 3, as follows:

Yeas— Messrs Grimes, Harris, Johnson, Williams, Grider, Bingham, Conkling, Boutwell, Blow and Rogers—10.

Nays— Messrs Howard and Stevens—2.

Absent— Messrs Fessenden, Washburne and Morrill—3.

So the motion to reconsider was agreed to.

And then, on motion of Mr. Grimes,

The Committee adjourned till Saturday next, at 10½ o'clock a.m.

——————— ———————

Washington April 28. 1866.

The Committee met pursuant to adjournment — all the members present.

The Chairman said that the vote of the Committee ordering the joint resolution and bill agreed upon to be reported to the two houses having been reconsidered at the last meeting, the Committee would resume the consideration of the same, and they would be regarded as still open to amendment.

Mr. Stevens moved to strike out all of section two of the proposed amendment to the Constitution of the United States, as follows:

"Sec. 2—From and after the fourth day of July, in the year 1876, no discrimination shall be made by any State, nor by the United States, as to the enjoyment by classes of persons of the right of suffrage, because of race, color, or previous condition of servitude."

And the following at the beginning of section three:

"Until the fourth day of July, 1876."

So that the third section would then read,

59

"No class of persons, as to the right of whom to suffrage discrimination shall be made by any State because of race, color or previous condition of servitude, shall be included in the basis of representation."

After discussion,

The question was taken and it was decided in the affirmative, yeas 12, nays 2, not voting 1, as follows;

Yeas — Messrs Grimes, Harris, Johnson, Williams, Stevens, Morrill, Grider, Bingham, Conkling, Boutwell, Blow and Rogers — 12.

Nays — Messrs Howard and Washburne — 2.

Not voting — The Chairman — 1.

So the motion to strike out was agreed to.

Mr Williams moved to strike out what had been section three, and to insert in lieu thereof the following;

"Representatives shall be apportioned among the several states which may be included within this Union according to their respective numbers, counting the whole number of persons in each State excluding Indians not taxed. But whenever in any State the elective franchise shall be denied to any portion of its male citizens, not less than twenty one years of age, or in any way abridged, except for participation in rebellion or other crime, the basis of representation in such State shall be reduced in the proportion which the number of such male citizens shall bear to the whole number of male citizens not less than twenty one years of age."

After discussion

The question was taken, and it was decided in the affirmative, yeas 12,

Grider, Bingham, Conkling, Boutwell, Blow and Rogers — 12.

Nays — Messrs Howard, Stevens and Washburne — 3.

So the motion of Mr. Williams was agreed to.

The Committee proceeded to consider the following section;

"Sec. 4 — Debts or obligations already incurred or which may hereafter be incurred in aid of insurrection or of war against the Union, and claims for compensation for loss of involuntary service or labor, shall not be paid by any State, nor by the United States."

Mr. Rogers moved to amend by striking out the words "by any State, nor."

The question was taken, and it was decided in the negative, yeas 3, nays 12, as follows;

Yeas — Messrs Johnson, Grider and Rogers — 3.

Nays — The Chairman, Messrs Grimes, Harris, Howard, Williams, Stevens, Washburne, Morrill, Bingham, Conkling, Boutwell and Blow — 12.

So the amendment was rejected.

Mr. Bingham moved to change the phraseology of the section, so that it should read;

"Neither the United States nor any state shall assume or pay any debt or obligation already incurred, or which may hereafter be incurred, in aid of insurrection or of war against the United States, or any claim for compensation for loss of involuntary service or labor.

The motion was agreed to.

Mr. Boutwell moved to insert the following as an additional section;

Sec — The President and Vice President of the late Confederate States of America so-called; the heads of departments thereof; those who in other countries acted as agents of the Confederate States of America so called; those who having been heads of departments of the United States, or officers of the army or navy of the United States, or members of either house of the 36th Congress of the United States, afterwards aided in the late rebellion; and any one who as governor of either of the so-called Confederate States gave aid or comfort to the late rebellion, are declared to be forever ineligible to any office under the United States."

Mr. Stevens moved to amend the section proposed by Mr. Boutwell by inserting after the clause relating to confederate agents in foreign countries the following:

"officers of the army or navy of the Confederate States of America so-called, above the rank of colonel in the army or master in the navy."

After discussion,

The question was taken and it was decided in the negative, yeas 3, nays 12, as follows:

Yeas—Messrs Stevens, Washburne and Conkling—3.

Nays—The Chairman, Messrs Grimes, Harris, Howard, Johnson, Williams, Morrill, Grider, Bingham, Boutwell, Blow and Rogers—12.

So the amendment of Mr. Stevens was not agreed to.

The question was then taken upon the section proposed by Mr. Boutwell, and it was decided in the negative, yeas 6, nays 8, not voting 1, as follows:

Yeas—Messrs Harris, Stevens, Washburne, Morrill, Conkling and Boutwell—6.

Mr. Harris moved to insert the following as an additional section, to follow the section in relation to representation;

"Sec—Until the fourth day of July, in the year 1870, all persons who voluntarily adhered to the late insurrection, giving it aid and comfort, shall be excluded from the right to vote for Representatives in Congress and for electors for President and Vice President of the United States."

After discussion.

The question was taken, and it was decided in the negative, yeas 7, nays 8, as follows;

Yeas— Messrs Harris, Howard, Stevens, Washburne, Morrill, Conkling and Boutwell—7.

Nays—The Chairman, Messrs Grimes, Johnson, Williams, Grider, Bingham, Blow and Rogers—8.

So the section proposed by Mr. Harris was not agreed to.

Subsequently, after discussion,

Mr. Grimes moved to reconsider the vote by which the section proposed by Mr. Harris was rejected.

The question was taken, and it was decided in the affirmative, yeas 8, nays 5, not voting 2, as follows;

Yeas— The Chairman, Messrs Grimes, Harris, Howard, Stevens, Morrill, Conkling and Boutwell—8.

who had temporarily left the committee room.

The question recurred upon agreeing to the section proposed by Mr. Harris.

The question was taken, and it was decided in the affirmative, yeas 7, nays 6, not voting 2, as follows:

Yeas — Messrs Grimes, Harris, Howard, Stevens, Morrill, Conkling and Boutwell — 7.

Nays — The Chairman, Messrs Johnson, Grider, Bingham, Blow and Rogers — 6.

Not voting — Messrs Williams and Washburne — 2.

So the section was adopted.

The section granting power to Congress to enforce the provisions of the article was adopted.

Mr Bingham moved to strike out the first section of the proposed amendment to the Constitution, which was as follows:

"Section 1 — No discrimination shall be made by any State, or by the United States, as to the civil rights of persons, because of race, color, or previous condition of servitude."

and to insert in lieu thereof the following:

"Sec. 1 — No State shall make or enforce any law which shall abridge the privileges or immunities of citizens of the United States; nor shall any State deprive any person of life, liberty, or property without due process of law nor deny to any person within its jurisdiction the equal protection of the laws."

After discussion,

tive, yeas 10, nays 3, not voting 2, as follows;

Yeas— Messrs Johnson, Williams, Stevens, Washburne, Grider, Bingham, Conk ling, Boutwell, Blow and Rogers—10.

Nays—Messrs Grimes, Howard and Morrill—3.

Not voting—The Chairman and Mr. Harris—2.

So the motion of Mr. Bingham was agreed to.

The Committee then proceeded to the consideration of the bill to provide for restoring to the states lately in insurrection their full political rights.

Mr. Boutwell moved that that portion relating to certain persons to be excluded from office be considered as a separate bill.

The motion was agreed to.

The preamble was modified, in so far as it recites the proposed amendment to the Constitution to correspond with the action of the Committee this morning.

The Committee proceeded to consider the following section;

"Be it enacted, etc. That whenever the above recited amendment shall have become part of the Constitution of the United States, and any State lately in insurrection shall have ratified the same and shall have modified its constitution and laws in conformity with the first section thereof, the senators and representatives from such state if found, duly elected and qualified, shall after having taken the required oaths of office, be admitted into Congress as such.

Mr. Boutwell moved to amend the section by striking out all after the word "That" and inserting the following:

"whenever the above recited amendment shall have become a part of the Constitution of the United States, and whenever either Tennessee or Arkansas shall have ratified the same, and shall have so modified its constitution and laws as to make them conform thereto, and shall have provided a system of equal suffrage for all loyal male citizens within its jurisdiction who are not less than twenty one years of age, the Senators and Representatives from such state, if found duly elected and qualified, shall after having taken the required oaths of office, be admitted into Congress as such; provided that nothing contained in this act shall be so construed as to disfranchise any loyal person now entitled to vote"

Mr. Bingham moved to amend the amendment by striking out all the first part to and including the words "the same" and inserting — "whenever either Tennessee or Arkansas shall have ratified the above recited amendment".

After discussion,

The question was taken upon the amendment to the amendment, and it was decided in the negative, yeas 4, nays 7, not voting 4, as follows:

Yeas — Messrs Johnson, Williams, Bingham and Blow — 4.

Nays — The Chairman, Messrs Grimes, Howard, Stevens, Morrill, Grider and Rogers — 7.

Not voting — Messrs Harris, Washburne, Conkling and Boutwell — 4.

So the amendment to the amendment was not agreed to.

The question was then taken upon the amendment of Mr. Boutwell, and it was decided in the negative, yeas 2, nays 9, not voting 4, as follows:

Yeas — Messrs Johnson and Boutwell — 2.

Nays — The Chairman, Messrs Grimes, Howard, Williams, Stevens, Grider, Bingham, Blow and Rogers — 9

not voting — Messrs Harris, Washburne, Morrill and Conkling — 4.

So the amendment was not agreed to.

Mr. Conkling moved to amend the first section of the bill under consideration by striking out the words "with the first section thereof", and inserting the word "therewith" in lieu thereof.

The amendment was agreed to.

Mr. Williams moved to amend by striking out all after the words "That whenever" and inserting the following:

"any one of the states lately in rebellion shall ratify the above-recited amendment as required by the Constitution of the United States, the Senators and Representatives of such state shall after the 4th day of March, 1867, if found duly elected and qualified and after taking the required oaths of office, be admitted into Congress as such: Provided that Senators and Representatives from Tennessee and Arkansas, elected and qualified as aforesaid, shall be admitted into Congress as soon as said states respectively shall ratify said amendment as aforesaid."

After discussion,

The question was taken, and it was decided in the negative, yeas 4, nays 9, not voting 2, as follows:

Yeas — Messrs Johnson, Williams, Bingham and Blow — 4.

Nays — The Chairman, Messrs Grimes, Howard, Stevens, Morrill, Grider, Conkling, Boutwell and Rogers — 9.

Not voting — Messrs Harris and Washburne — 2.

So the amendment was not agreed to.

The first section as amended was then agreed to.

The second section in relation to the direct tax was agreed to.

The Committee then proceeded to consider the bill declaring certain persons ineligible to office.

The first part was as follows;

Be it enacted etc. that no person shall be eligible to either branch of the National Legislature who is included in any of the following classes; namely."

Mr. Conkling moved to amend by striking out the words "either branch of the National Legislature" and inserting the words "any office under the government of the United States".

The amendment was agreed to.

The next clause was as follows;

"First — The President and Vice President of the Confederate States of America so-called, the heads of departments and members of both houses of Congress thereof."

The Chairman moved to amend by striking out the words "and members of both houses of Congress".

The question was taken, and it was decided in the affirmative, yeas

So the amendment was agreed to.

The next clause was as follows;

'Second — Those who in other countries acted as agents of the Confederate States of America so-called'.

Mr. Howard moved to strike it out.

The question was taken, and it was decided in the negative, yeas 3. nays 12. as follows;

Yeas — Messrs Howard, Grider and Rogers — 3.

Nays — The Chairman, Messrs Grimes, Harris, Johnson. Williams, Stevens, Washburne, Morrill, Bingham, Conkling, Boutwell & Blow — 12.

So the motion to strike out was not agreed to.

The next clause was as follows;

'Third — Heads of departments in the Government of the United State officers of the army and navy of the United States, Judges of the Courts of the United States, and members of either house of the 36th Congress of the United State who aided the late rebellion.

Mr. Grimes moved to amend by inserting before the word "Judges", the words "and all persons educated at the naval or military academy of the United

Mr. Grimes moved to amend by striking out the words—"Those who acted as officers of the Confederate States of America so called, above the grade of colonel in the army or master in the navy, and."

After discussion,

The question was taken, and it was decided in the negative, yeas 4, nays 11, as follows;

Yeas— Messrs Grimes, Johnson, Grider and Rogers — 4.

Nays— The Chairman, Messrs Harris, Howard, Williams, Stevens, Washburne, Morrill, Bingham, Conkling, Boutwell and Blow — 11.

So the amendment was not agreed to.

The next clause was agreed to as follows;

"Fifth— Those who have treated officers or soldiers or sailors of the army or navy of the United States, captured during the late war, otherwise than lawfully as prisoners of war."

Mr. Grider submitted the following resolutions;

Resolved, That in the opinion of this Committee, the people of Tennessee having elected according to law loyal men as Senators and Representatives, they should be admitted to seats in the present Congress upon taking the usual oath of office.

Resolved further, That each of the states not now represented should be allowed representation upon the same terms.

Mr. Grimes moved to amend the first resolution by adding thereto the

The question was taken, and it was decided in the affirmative, yeas 9. nays 4. not voting 2. as follows;

Yeas— The Chairman, Messrs Grimes, Harris, Howard, Williams, Stevens, Morrill, Bingham and Conkling—9.

Nays— Messrs Johnson, Grider, Blow and Rogers—4.

Not voting— Messrs Washburne and Boutwell—2.

So the amendment was agreed to.

Mr. Stevens moved to lay the resolutions on the table.

The question was taken, and it was decided in the negative, yeas 5, nays 7, not voting 3, as follows;

Yeas— Messrs Howard, Williams, Stevens, Morrill and Bingham—5.

Nays— Messrs Grimes, Harris, Johnson, Grider, Conkling, Blow and Rogers—7.

Not voting— The Chairman, Messrs Washburne and Boutwell—3.

So the motion to lay on the table was not agreed to.

The question recurred upon agreeing to the resolutions as amended.

The question was taken, and it was decided in the negative, yeas 2, nays 10, not voting 3, as follows;

Yeas— Messrs Grimes and Johnson—2.

Nays— Messrs Harris, Howard, Williams, Stevens, Morrill, Grider, Bingham, Conkling, Blow and Rogers—10

Not voting— The Chairman, Messrs Washburne and Boutwell—3.

So the resolutions were not adopted.

Mr. Stevens moved that the joint resolution and bills adopted by the committee to-day be reported on Monday next to the two houses of Congress, and that leave be asked to submit at some future time reports to accompany the same.

Mr. Boutwell asked that a separate vote be taken upon the joint resolution and bills; which was ordered.

The first question was upon reporting the joint resolution proposing an amendment to the Constitution of the United States.

The question was taken, and it was decided in the affirmative, yeas 12, nays 3, as follows;

Yeas — The Chairman, Messrs Grimes, Harris, Howard, Williams, Stevens, Washburne, Morrill, Bingham, Conkling, Boutwell and Blow — 12.

Nays — Messrs Johnson, Grider and Rogers — 3.

So the motion to report the joint resolution was agreed to.

The next question was upon reporting the bill to provide for restoring to the States lately in insurrection their full political rights.

The question was taken, and it was decided in the affirmative, yeas 12, nays 3, as follows;

Yeas — The Chairman, Messrs Grimes, Harris, Howard, Williams, Stevens, Washburne, Morrill, Bingham, Conkling, Boutwell and Blow — 12.

Nays — Messrs Johnson, Grider and Rogers — 3.

So the motion was agreed to.

nays — Messrs Johnson, Grider and Rogers — 3.

So the motion was agreed to.

On motion of Mr. Rogers, it was

Ordered that the minority of the Committee have leave to submit minority reports.

On motion of Mr. Grimes, it was

Ordered, That the injunction of secrecy be removed, so far as relates to the results of the action of the Committee at this session.

On motion of Mr. Boutwell it was

Ordered, That the stenographer of this Committee be authorized to furnish to the agent of the Associated press, and the correspondents of such newspapers as may apply to him, copies of the joint resolution and bills adopted by the Committee to-day, after the same shall have been submitted to and approved by the Chairman.

The joint resolution and bills adopted are as follows;

A joint resolution proposing an amendment to the Constitution of the United States.

Be it resolved by the Senate and House of Representatives of the United States of America in Congress assembled (two thirds of both Houses concurring,) That the following article be proposed to the Legislatures of the several States as an amendment to the Constitution of the United States, which, when ratified by three fourths of said Legislatures, shall be valid as part of the Constitution, namely:

Article —

Sec. 1. No state shall make or enforce any law which shall abridge the privileges or immunities of citizens of the United States; nor shall any State deprive any person of life, liberty, or property without due process of law; nor deny to any person within its jurisdiction the equal protection of the laws.

Sec. 2. Representatives shall be apportioned among the several States which may be included within this Union according to their respective numbers, counting the whole number of persons in each State, excluding Indians not taxed. But whenever in any State the elective franchise shall be denied to any portion of its male citizens not less than twenty-one years of age, or in any way abridged, except for participation in rebellion or other crime, the basis of representation in such State shall be reduced in the proportion which the number of male citizens shall bear to the whole number of such male citizens not less than twenty-one years of age.

Sec. 3. Until the 4th day of July, in the year 1870, all persons who voluntarily adhered to the late insurrection, giving it aid and comfort, shall be excluded from the right to vote for Representatives in Congress and for electors for President and Vice President of the United States.

Sec. 4. Neither the United States nor any State shall assume or pay any debt or obligation already incurred, or which may hereafter be incurred, in aid of insurrection or of war against the United States, or any claim for compensa-

A bill to provide for restoring to the States lately in insurrection their full political rights.

Whereas it is expedient that the States lately in insurrection should, at the earliest day consistent with the future peace and safety of the Union, be restored to full participation in all political rights; and whereas the Congress did, by joint resolution, propose for ratification to the Legislatures of the several States, as an amendment to the Constitution of the United States, an article in the following words, to wit:

"Article —

"Sec. 1. No State shall make or enforce any law which shall abridge the privileges or immunities of citizens of the United States; nor shall any State deprive any person of life, liberty, or property without due process of law; nor deny to any person within its jurisdiction the equal protection of the laws."

"Sec. 2. Representatives shall be apportioned among the several States which may be included within this Union, according to their respective numbers, counting the whole number of persons in each State, excluding Indians not taxed. But whenever, in any State, the elective franchise shall be denied to any portion of its male citizens not less than twenty-one years of age, or in any way abridged except for participation in rebellion or other crime, the basis of representation in such State shall be reduced in the proportion which the number of such male citizens shall bear to the whole number of male citizens not less than twenty-one years of age.

Sec. 3. Until the 4th day of July, in the year 1870, all persons who voluntarily adhered to the late insurrection, giving it aid and comfort, shall be excluded from the right to vote for Representatives in Congress. and for electors for President and Vice President of the United States.

"Sec. 4. Neither the United States nor any State shall assume or pay any debt or obligation already incurred, or which may hereafter be incurred, in aid of insurrection or of war against the United States, or any claim for compensation for loss of involuntary service or labor.

"Sec. 5. The Congress shall have power to enforce, by appropriate legislation, the provisions of this article".

Now, therefore,

Be it enacted by the Senate and House of Representatives of the United States of America in Congress assembled, That whenever the above-recited amendment shall have become part of the Constitution of the United States, and any State lately in insurrection shall have ratified the same, and shall have modified its constitution and laws in conformity therewith, the Senators and Representatives from such State, if found duly elected and qualified, may, after having taken the required oaths of office, be admitted into Congress as such.

Sec. 2. And be it further enacted, That when any State lately in insurrection shall have ratified the foregoing amendment to the Constitution, any part of the direct tax under the act of August 5, 1861, which may remain due and unpaid in such State may be assumed and paid by such State; and the payment thereof, upon proper assurances from such State to be given to the Secretary of the Treasury of the United States, may be postponed for a period not exceeding ten years from and after the passage of this act.

A bill declaring certain persons ineligible to office under the Government of the United States.

Be it enacted by the Senate and House of Representatives of the United States of America in Congress assembled, That no person shall be eligible to any office under the Government of the United States who is included in any of the following classes, namely:

1. The President and Vice President of the Confederate States of America, so called, and the heads of departments thereof.

2. Those who in other countries acted as agents of the Confederate States of America, so called.

3. Heads of Departments of the United States, officers of the Army and Navy of the United States, and all persons educated at the Military or Naval Academy of the United States, judges of the courts of the United States, and members of either House of the Thirty-Sixth Congress of the United States, who gave aid or comfort to the late rebellion.

4. Those who acted as officers of the Confederate States of America, so called, above the grade of colonel in the army or master in the navy, and any one who, as Governor of either of the so-called Confederate States, gave aid or comfort to the rebellion.

5. Those who have treated officers or soldiers or sailors of the Army or Navy of the United States, captured during the late war, otherwise than law-

Washington, June 6, 1866.

The Committee met pursuant to the call of its Chairman — Absent — Messrs Washburne, Blow, Rogers, Johnson, Grider and Conkling.

The Chairman stated that he had called the Committee together for the purpose of laying before them a report he had prepared to accompany the measures which at the last meeting the Committee directed to be reported to the two houses of Congress.

The report was read and adopted.

On motion of Mr. Howard,

The Chairmen of the Senate and House portions of the Joint Committee were instructed to submit the report just adopted to their respective houses.

Adjourned to meet on call of the Chairman.

Attest
(Sgd) Wm Blair Lord.
Clerk.

<u>Second Session.</u>

In the House of Representatives
December 4th 1866.

Resolved, (the Senate concurring) That the Joint Committee of Fifteen on Reconstruction, appointed during the last session of Congress, shall be reappointed under the same rules and regulations as then existed, and that all the documents and resolutions which were referred then be now considered as referred to them anew.

Attest

Edwd. McPherson.
Clerk.

In the Senate of the United States
December 5, 1866.

Resolved, That the Senate concur in the foregoing resolution of the House of Representatives, relative to the reappointment of the Joint Committee of Fifteen on Reconstruction.

Attest

J. W. Forney
Secretary.
by W. J. McDonald.
Chief Clerk.

Office House of Representatives U.S.
February 15th, 1867.

I certify that the foregoing is a true copy of the original now on file in this office.

Attest

Edwd. Mc Pherson
Clerk.

Members on the part of the Senate.

Mr. William E. Fessenden   of   Maine.

"   James W. Grimes   "   Iowa .

.   Ira Harris   .   New York .

.   Jacob M. Howard   .   Ohio.

"   Reverdy Johnson   "   Maryland .

and   .   George C. Williams   .   Oregon.

Members on the part of the House of Reps.

Mr. Thaddeus Stevens   of   Penna.

"   John F. Farnsworth   "   Ills. vice Mr. Washburne excused.

"   Justin S. Morrill   .   Vermont .

Elijah Hise   "   Kentucky vice Mr. Grider deceased.

"   John A. Bingham   "   Ohio.

"   Roscoe Conkling   .   New York.

"   George S. Boutwell   Mass.

"   Henry T. Blow   Missouri

and   .   Andrew J. Rogers   .   New Jersey.

Washington Feb. 2. 1867.

The Committee met on call of the Chairman at Senate Committee Room on the Pacific Rail-road. Present Mr. Fessenden (Chairman) and the entire Committee.

On motion of *Mr. Stevens*, House Bill (Substitute for House Bill No. 543) was read, when,

On motion of *Mr. Bingham*, the original Bill was also read — After reference had been made to both bills, *Mr. Stevens*, submitted the following resolution,

"That the States lately in Rebellion shall be reconstructed upon the principle of granting them enabling Acts to form their State Constitutions,"

which after some discussion, was modified by him on leave as follows;

"That the States lately in Rebellion shall be reconstructed upon the principle, "*providing by Act of Congress that they may form State Constitutions and Governments*.

The discussion upon this motion was continued by Messrs Stevens, Howard Bingham, Conkling, Johnson, Williams, Farnsworth and Boutwell, during which time, *Mr. Bingham* asked leave to amend the Original House Bill No. 543, as follows, add after word, "therewith", the following. "And shall have secured impartial suffrage to the male citizens of the U.S. of full age resident therein", the section amended reading as follows:

"Be it enacted by the Senate and House of Representatives of the United States of America in Congress assembled, That whenever the above-recited amendment shall have become part of the Constitution of the United States, and any State lately in insurrection shall have ratified the same, and shall have modified its constitution and laws in conformity therewith, and shall have secured impartial suffrage to the male citizens of the United States, of full age resident therein, the senators and representatives from such State, if found duly elected and qualified, may, after having taken the required oaths of office, be admitted into Congress as such.

Pending discussion of Mr. Stevens' Resolution, it being near 12 o'clock,

On motion of <u>Mr. Howard</u> the Committee adjourned to meet on Wednesday morning next at 10 o'clock.

——————

Wednesday, Febry. 6th 1867.

The Committee met pursuant to adjournment. Present - The Chairman, Messrs Grimes, Harris, Howard, Johnson, Williams, Stevens, Farnsworth, Morrill, Bingham, Conkling, Boutwell and Blow.

Absent - Messrs Hise and Rogers.

On motion of the <u>Chairman</u>, Geo. A. Mark was appointed as clerk to the Committee.

On motion of the <u>Chairman</u>, it was agreed that the proceedings of the Committee should be considered as secret and confidential.

<u>Mr. Conkling</u> moved that the further consideration of pending resolution be postponed, and Senate Bill 564 be taken up.

The motion was agreed to.

After reading of S.B. 564 by the Chairman, Mr. Conkling presented the same with amendments.

The Committee then proceeded to the consideration of the preamble, and the several sections of the bill.

word, "Congress", in the fourth line, "and without the sanction of the people".

The amendment was agreed to.

It was also agreed to strike out in the fifth line, the words, "and therefore are of no constitutional validity"

Mr. Farnsworth moved to insert after the word, "whereas", the words, "said pretended governments", striking out down to the word, "afford", in the seventh line so that it would read, "and whereas said pretended governments afford &c".

The question was taken by yeas and nays, and it was decided in the affirmative — Yeas 8 — Nays 5 — Absent 2.

Yeas — The Chairman, Messrs Grimes, Harris, Johnson, Farnsworth, Morrill, Bingham and Blow — 8.

Nays — Messrs Howard, Williams, Stevens, Conkling and Boutwell — 5.

Absent — Messrs Rogers and Hise — 2.

So the amendment was agreed to.

Mr. Johnson moved to further amend, by striking out in the eighth line, the words, "but countenance and encourage lawlessness and crime".

The amendment was not agreed to.

In the eleventh line it was agreed to amend by striking out the word, "formed", and inserting the word "established".

Mr Bingham offered the following as a substitute for the preamble, viz:

"Whereas it is necessary, that peace and good order should be enforced in the several states of Virginia, North Carolina, South Carolina, Georgia, Mississippi, Alabama, Louisiana, Florida, Texas and Arkansas, lately in rebellion, until said states shall be fully restored to their constitutional relations to the Government of the United States.

The question was taken by yeas and nays, and it was decided in the negative. Yeas 4. Nays 9. Absent 2.

Yeas. Messrs Grimes, Johnson, Bingham and Blow. 4.

Nays. The Chairman, Messrs Harris, Howard, Williams, Stevens, Farnsworth, Morrill, Conkling and Boutwell. 9.

Absent. Messrs Rogers and Hise. 2.

So the substitute of Mr. Bingham was not agreed to.

The Committee next proceeded to the consideration of the first section, amended by Mr. Conkling, so that after the enacting clause, it should read as follows.

"That said so-called states shall be divided into military districts and made subject to the military authority of the United States as hereinafter prescribed and for that purpose Virginia shall constitute the first district; North Carolina and South Carolina the second district; Georgia, Alabama and Florida the third district; Mississippi and Arkansas the fourth district; and Louisiana and Texas the fifth district."

Mr. Bingham moved to amend the section as amended by substituting after the enacting clause the following.

"That said states be divided into five military districts as follows" &c.

The question was taken by yeas and nays and it was decided in the negative. Yeas 2. Nays 9. Absent or not voting 4.

Yeas. Messrs Johnson and Bingham. 2.

Nays. The Chairman, Messrs Harris, Howard, Stevens, Farnsworth, Morrill, Conkling, Boutwell and Blow. 9.

Absent or not voting. Messrs Grimes, Williams, Rogers and Hise. 4.

So the amendment of Mr. Bingham was not agreed to.

Mr. Bingham moved to amend by striking out in the third line the word, "so-called".

The amendment was not agreed to.

The question then recurred upon the adoption of the section as amended by Mr. Conkling,

And the section was adopted.

The amendments to the second section submitted by Mr. Conkling were agreed to and the section read as follows –

"Sec. 2. And be it further enacted, That it shall be the duty of the General of the army, under the authority of the President, to assign to the command of each of said districts an officer of the regular army, not below the rank of brigadier general, and to detail a sufficient military force to enable such officer to perform his duties and enforce his authority within the district to which he is assigned".

The third section was then taken up, and after discussion,

Mr. Harris moved to amend by striking out in the sixth line the word "local" and insert the word "civil".

The amendment was agreed to.

Mr. Bingham moved to amend by striking out in the second and third lines the words, "peaceable and law abiding".

The amendment was agreed to.

Mr. Bingham moved further to amend by inserting in line nine, after the word "tribunals", the words, "in the mode prescribed by existing laws for courts-martial".

the eleventh line, the word "local".

The amendment was not agreed to.

And the section as amended was then adopted.

The amendments to section four submitted by Mr. Conkling were agreed to, and the section read as follows —

"Sec. 4. And be it further enacted, That courts and judicial officers of the United States shall not issue writs of habeas corpus in behalf of persons in military custody, unless some commissioned officer on duty in the district wherein the person is detained shall indorse upon said petition a statement certifying, upon honor, that he has knowledge, or information, as to the cause and circumstances of the alleged detention, and that he believes the same to be wrongful; and further that he believes that the indorsed petition is preferred in good faith, and in furtherance of justice, and not to hinder or delay the punishment of crime. All persons put under military arrest by virtue of this act shall be tried without unnecessary delay, and no cruel or unusual punishment shall be inflicted."

And the section as amended was adopted.

The amendments to Section five, as proposed by Mr. Conkling were agreed to, and it then read as follows:

"Sec. 5. And be it further enacted, That no sentence of any military commission or tribunal hereby authorized, affecting the life or liberty of any person, shall be executed until it is approved by the officer in command of the district, and the laws and regulations for the government of the army shall not be affected by this act except in so far as they conflict with its provisions."

And the section was adopted as amended.

Mr. Howard moved to further amend the second section, by striking out in the second and third lines, the words, "under the authority of the President".

After discussion the amendment of Mr. Howard was agreed to.

Mr. Harris moved that the Chairmen of the Senate and House portions of the Committee report the bill to their respective bodies.

The motion was not agreed to.

It was then moved that Mr. Stevens report the bill as amended to the House.

The motion was agreed to.

Mr. Bingham moved to report back to the House the bill previously reported.

The motion was not agreed to.

After-discussion, the Committee adjourned to meet on Saturday next at 10 o'clock.

Saturday, February 9. 1867.

The Committee met pursuant to adjournment.

Present- The Chairman. Messrs Williams, Bingham, Boutwell and Blow.

A quorum not being present the Committee adjourned to meet on call of the Chairman.

Geo. A. Marr
Clerk.